IF YOU LIKE DIFFICULTY

Harbor Mountain Press acknowledges the support of
Pentangle Council on the Arts (Woodstock, Vermont)
for this and other literary projects.

First printing 2007

ISBN 0-9786009-6-7

Series Editor:
Peter Money

Cover illustration:
Harley Terra Candella
www.terracandella.com

Production editing:
Barbara Jones

Harbor Mountain Press
Brownsville, Vermont
0 5 0 3 7

www.harbormountainpress.com

IF YOU LIKE DIFFICULTY

Jan Clausen

Harbor Mountain Press
Brownsville, Vermont

ACKNOWLEDGMENTS

I am immoderately grateful to my dear friends Bea Gates, Elena Georgiou, Joan Larkin, and Steve Turtell. More times than I can count, a scheduled meeting of our poetry group has nudged me to "try to write *something*," secure in the anticipation of meticulous close readings, warm encouragement, good food, and world-class literary gossip.

I am also grateful to the New York Foundation for the Arts for a poetry fellowship awarded me in 2003, and to the directors of Norcroft and Centrum for writing residencies during which several of the poems in this book took shape.

Working with Harbor Mountain Press has been a gratifying and remarkably humane experience. My thanks to Peter Money for strong editorial support and great e-mails, to Barbara Jones for design expertise and patience, and to Harley Terra Candella for permission to use his work on the cover.

I extend my thanks to the editors of the literary magazines, webzines, and anthologies in which some of these poems first appeared: *Big Bridge, BigCityLit.com, Bloom, Coconut, CrossConnect, Fence, Gargoyle, Hamilton Stone Review, Margie, Nightsun, North American Review, Ploughshares, Red, White, & Blues: Poetic Vistas on the Promise of America,* and *Tribes.*

CONTENTS

Voxology

To Victor H. Clausen, 1924–2007

into hardest nature

ab·la·tion (ă-blā´shən) *n.* **1.** Surgical excision or amputation of a body part or tissue. **2.** The erosive processes by which a glacier is reduced. **3.** *Aerospace.* The dissipation of heat generated by atmospheric friction, especially in the atmospheric reentry of a spacecraft or missile, by means of a melting heat shield. [Late Latin *ablātiō, ablātiōn-,* from Latin *ablātus,* past participle of *auferre,* to carry away: *ab-,* away: see AB-[1] + *lātus,* carried; see **telə–** in Appendix.]

—*The American Heritage Dictionary*

VOXOLOGY

VOXOLOGY

I.

Language was lying around
she picked some up

she smeared it on her breast
or was it brain

it wouldn't let her off the line
it wouldn't let her off the hook

you have a voice
you have a voice they said

she *was* more than a fleshfold!

call her   Vocalia

~

who tittered at sallies
clappt her backside down

strode
strident

text messaging stuff like

3

OURBO
DIESOUR
LIVESOUR
RITE2
DEICIDE

~

VOXY LADY!
tampon poetess

undertook a journey to the bottom of the flesh
in what manner of bathysphere

while trying to KEEP AN EYE
ON BIG PICTURE

mooned masses
on pirate frequencies

her scatterings of masticated voicings
dribbled round the perimeter

II.

Something had happened
to magnify debasement

(Nipple confusion might have been an issue.)

(The fact that caring had not been demonstrated.)

Ms. Lack
got down
on all fours

kindled
keened
crept
while feeling sorta
language-y

reared up chiding
tearing
something in teeth

    (HOW DO I STACK UP?
    revolved   recurred)

but practiced

silence
cunning
blogging

deep
in the heart
of nope

blasted
caddywompus

howled
awry

VOXATION
IS MINE
saith Vocalia

~

HER ACTUAL STRUGGLE

struck them as

comeuppance

HER ACTUAL STRUGGLE

struck them as

commonplace

a throwback

to the scrap heap

careless dung

HER ACTUAL STRUGGLE

struck them as

delicious

baldly buxom

bovine-bloviant

(like putting

lipstick on a

lip

repeatedly)

HER ACTUAL STRUGGLE

to alchemize

syntax

out of

just

feeling

out of just

feeling

fuckd

over

& over

again

~

Vocalia felt
so *over*
the whole charade

she bayed
at the cosmic fucker

THOU HAST
GIVEN ME A

vOICE   BOX

~

she finds

she rhymes

with naught

between

below

that fuzzy

gulch

the zilch

epitome

~

babababab
arrarrarara

someone was
verging
on
speaking

Vocalia
velcro'd
the Pamper
& was still

~

heard

=

herd   (repeatedly)

~

her blowzy throes
compounded
took the cake

9

in tufts of
dithyramb &
curettage

dulcet
rattletrap
whimpers

riled
utterance

the earlessness
was frankly epochal

like putting lipstick on a
prick

the grooves
of boydom
rang

with din of
raining on
the whole shebang

~

what

ululates
pullulates
ovulates
vulvulates

so

& just keeps hitting *PUBLISH*

~

be

hold

Her

Immanence

warlit

scavenges

orificial

oracle

or

or

~

"people don't dig
her *freaky old voice*
well I think it's beautiful"—

squawk–whispered   *you don't know what love is*

groaned home
in droves

~

echolalia
persisting

would've offed
a lesser
evil

~

so she became an artist

after a while

HAPPENSTANCE

GHAZAL: HAPPENSTANCE

Ghazal: in Arabic: whispering words of love or
cry of a gazelle cornered in hunt

I sat in my house and waited for something to happen.
Life's drapery so smooth, I hankered for rumpling to happen.

Ten thousand verses like devil-ridden swine!
It's po month. Lyric trampling can happen.

The young in one another's spoken word—
their hope's for better sampling to happen.

"Shit happens," snaps a T-shirt. "Suck it up."
Sans attitude, could Gotham clothing happen?

Tulips Are in the Cooler, reads a sign.
Crank fridges high, let global warming happen.

Sue's Shih Tzu died last Tuesday. She's a wreck
but his DNA's iced, so eventual cloning can happen.

One Broadway mom's stroller flies an Israeli flag.
From "Baby on Board" to a nod for Sharoning to happen.

Shun passive verbs. Say who did what to whom.
You might get textual mattering to happen.

They sold their farms, prayed aloud on a holy hill.
What now? The Second Coming didn't happen.

Bushwhacked? Attack. God's country gets it done,
still waiting for the vision thing to happen.

I marched, but wouldn't chant, "We are all Palestinian,"
a holdout for the precision thing to happen.

Did you ever dream lucky, wake up cold in hand?
Must be your fault. How'd you let that thieving happen?

My girl-grandmother bucks for a break in barbarian pines,
cell-bent on compelling life's boreal blooming to happen.

Orange butterfly rides like a bow on a gift-wrap of flies.
Moist scat-table set in the road for their feasting to happen.

In anguish-etched close-up, the family plugs lethal injection:
Give us our closure—*he* made the bereaving happen.

From Gujarat, Miss.: charred, hell-hacked sentience.
We're history. We make the howling happen.

Mossed tombstones remind us, in quaint theological guise:
To you, too, this no-thing, the one truly new thing, must happen.

He/she-ing, the we-beasts keep boarding the narrative ark.
Dark arc. And its desolate solace: offspring (still) happen.

I've days when I manage to think like a bug in the sun;
a stone on the shore, in whose cove-home great harboring happens.

Not Jew, Jenin—but, Jan, you're next of kin.
Let your epitaph read: *Happy poet—she made nothing happen.*

Brooklyn, New York and the North Shore of Lake Superior
April-June, 2002

15

IF YOU SEE SOMETHING, SAY SOMETHING

Stand, walk, run, eat, show movies or move or be moved by some
thing *rather than oneself.* —Yvonne Rainer

I should/I don't want to:
that old senseless split, harking
back to childhood.

Sun's impersonal keystroke.
Blue ledge of air.

He grills me about what I saw in Africa.

Pyramids
of shaved oranges
(someone's livelihood)
disclosed by a smoking wick.
Kid down on all fours
being stomach sick
into a pungent ditch.
In Cape Coast,
this was.

Don't want to— ?
Help.
Or if one can't?

Be moved
by patterns blazing
at cross purposes. Normal accidents.
The wild thing,
so-called.

On the cherry esplanade, a single tree
has bungled time.
It fastens this mussed
and tentative corsage
to December's warm lapel.

Must I grieve then
or what?

Run riot.
Keep shop.

Tiny crimson apple berried branches.

One might devise a sequence.
Tunnel into the everyday.
Register the old-fashioned self's
bleeding out
into anyone.

Still.
It was me, seeing.
I'm stuck.

Blunder through
the rose garden without the roses.

Stumble. Rummage. Scribble. Pluck. Plummet
into the gorgeous cleft
between picture
and narrative
world without end.

It's true.
There's nothing for it.

Do a few things
and die.

NO MATTER WHO YOU VOTE FOR,
THE GOVERNMENT GETS IN

A baby cried, reminded me of death
in the midst of my headache walk.
Rough work to carve a self.
I pondered what to do.

In the midst of my headache walk,
the evening lamps were lit.
I pondered what to do.
The street glowed softly white

as the evening lamps were lit.
I checked my neighbors out.
The street glowed softly white
under blackly marshaled branches.

I checked my neighbors out;
perhaps they were doing rudeness.
Under blackly marshaled branches,
I saw slippery TV pictures.

Perhaps they were doing rudeness.
Homesick for scraps of my past,
I saw slippery TV pictures.
I saw the President's face.

Homesick for scraps of my past,
I beheld the world in its writhing.
I saw the President's face.
I spied the harsh bones of abandon.

I beheld the world in its writhing,
I felt tired of history.
I spied the harsh bones of abandon.
I felt like eating organic ice cream.

I felt tired of history.
So what else is new?
I felt like eating organic ice cream.
I felt like drinking Lethe water.

So what else is new?
Rough work to carve a self.
I felt like drinking Lethe water.
A baby cried.

TREATMENT

He says he tells his student, do a treatment! *The guy keeps writing* scenes!

FADE IN

INT. MINDSCAPE—NIGHT

Amalgam of cavelike Managua interiors
and shiftless New England farmsprawl.
Telephone knell (black rotary job from the fifties).

                    POET
It's the oneiric ringing again.

I.

I'm eating some raw, springy vegetable in a bowl, like a cross
between colorless, slimmed-down asparagus
and enormous bean sprouts laced with peanut sauce.
Every TV in the house works
except one. There's lots. This home
is vast: dim cluttered rooms conjoined,
ancestral seat of my arbitrary-only, fucked-up
Boymate Flesh the First. (Intercourse enters the picture.)
In the room I call mine, the channel-changing dial's
frozen thanks to a spoked array of toothpicks.
I can't dislodge the image in the box:
that sorrowing beagle visage
under the eave of Texas headgear.
Lyndon Johnson.
Lyndon Johnson.

21

~

Or I loll on the couch. (We called it a davenport.)
My therapist stands.
Her loosely belted bathrobe falls open more than once.
Embarrassment I manage to ignore.

~

In the Salvation Army Department Store
Reading Room, I make out
at a glance I'm at fault.
Graying, grungy savants lower up at me,
the contaminant feminine,
disrupter of their Readers
Digest Condensed
jouissance.

II.

Phoned Sara in Seattle.
Salmon battles. Dying
mothers of all her friends.
Folks living off the grid
doing diesel, wind farms
screwing up the view shed.
Whole lineages in thrall
to the Church of the Nazarene.
Their old rugged cross
blaring neon in the night
hauling fodder

to the godhead.
Take up your kilowatt hours,
follow me!

We met at an auction
of menses. Mine
have ceased.

III.

Shirking demonstrations, left sectarians
tiptoe into midday theaters, popcorn tubs in hand.
Sidle into the soft, greasy seats.
Streaming dreaming—what
could it wear away?

On screen, two outsized lovelies
in bed like night and day.
The one who might be "Spanish"
but can't remember her own name
inclines, heliotropic, over
the golden-girl-next-door type.

Later, they'll trade places.
And somebody meets—*a man!*
But right now, such gooey glory,
like birthday cake with breasts,
reiterated roses, ravenous peonies.

And here I come from people
who wouldn't buckle
to ravishing beauty
if it up and bit them.

IV.

Sensation that I'm leaving more and more behind.
Parents. Particulars. Yet—
how old potsherds gather consequence!
Merry Lynn Sponsler, who was "popular" (why?)
in kindergarten, wouldn't play with me.
I burned to be anointed by her blonde irrelevance—
adumbration of all these Tinkerbells of commerce.
All these talk show hosts of verse.

In a way, though, that book-besotted kid
who'd ditch her maidenhead
no longer interests me much.
Heaped self-detritus, port
from which I part
(we do, we must)—
to be lost.
To be everyone.

~

FADE IN

INT. MINDSCAPE—DAY

POET poetizes. Scatters
ashes in advance.

Toward the end
becoming husklike.

Then—something
about gender.

INSTEAD OF AN EPITHALAMION

Well we did our best in deracinated weather.
Daughters were wedding daughters, suddenly.
They'd registered at Bed Bath & Beyond.
Rain-hurled catalpa flowers bruised the yard.
The dual-mothered bride procured a dress,
to her surprise. Pert cannabis jungled up.
One wandered under oaks, umbrella'd to the hilt,
like some female in a lyric or a play,
the sort who'd *labor to be beautiful*,
forsooth. (That poet didn't do the math.)
Once mothers bedded down and chivvied death
(the "Great Behind"); now rivers hurry home
while marriage gathers its divorce-bouquet:
a shivaree of artless exes in the fray.

THE FATE OF FORMS

A field trip to the BMA back lot

Slumped on his nag, sad lord of disconsolate forms,
a graphically Vanquished white man's Indian
marshals the dream-array of refugees
impounded where museum parking lot
meets gated nature. Here is Loser Art:
plinth, bust, medallion, fractured bas-relief,
prow-nosed Ben Franklin, Neptune hoisting fork
caged cheek by jowl with wide-horned copper bull,
stout antique hydrants, street lamps felled like stiffs,
a minor, whale-girthed Lady Liberty.
Reiterated girls, dumped upside down,
rehearse a trite yet piteous appeal
ignored by youngsters posed near peonies
and seniors herded through the galleries.

POETRY IN MOTION

Sappho's wailing in the subway;
you can barely hear her lyre,
wedged between a boombox minstrel
and an expert on hellfire.

AT GODDARD

That blue plastic number
aluminum-armed and -legged

marooned where skeleton
grasses complement

the beachy pitch
of snow dunes (brown

too a winter color)
must be the Emily

Dickinson Chair
of Reclusive Poetics.

HOT BUTTON

So, she quips, you're back to realism!

Corn stubble swale, hill pale
First sight of brown bound I thought: dog
No—snow deer galumphing
(What did you expect, a bloody frangipani pulpit)

Let's just say I'm down
with repetition it's the gist of January
Slow chew of shaggy-legged lovelies
rayed out from the daily bale

It's dumping, we say
It's shaping works okay
Revelation of contour raining
limning weed stalks and headstones

(city people in headphones
simply zone the fuck out)
over backup wails of the damned:
snowmobiles

Crow a jet pronouncement

on the pallor underlying

something I was feeling

in the morning

maybe warning

sagging gables

off the night road

pack a skid of light, a bleed

Hoax repeats the parrot of my REM state

it's a step in language learning

letting me supply the meaning

Legal Load Limit: 24,000 Pounds

That's when I remember

winter is so fragile

just when I was racing

just when I was humming

just when I was ticking

just when I was kicking

crystal corset is relenting

narrow palette representing

icy stricture is expanding

Arctic bulwark only seeming

no more anything to lean on

than a myth on celluloid

What blankets us at best

a sort of mendicant request

a moth-eaten scrap

of old North

Under blur-moon, corrupt latitudes

cue tropic bludgeons

follow the money

warmward

Just when I was reeling dreaming back

PAGE TURNER

> *Of what consequence, though our planet explode,*
> *if there is no character involved in the explosion?*
> *In health we have not the least curiosity about*
> *such events. We do not live for idle amusement.*
> *I would not run round a corner to see the world*
> *blow up.*
> —Henry David Thoreau, "Life without Principle"

Late sedition in a bunker,
retribution in a hearse.
Rising action for the better,
resolution for the worse.

Metafiction in the basement,
jurisprudence in the trees.
Cacophonies of saviors
vend Cartesian prophecies.

Light sedation in a kill box,
exposition on the cross
where the Forest of Indifference
confronts the Sea of Loss.

Nonstop necklacing and fragging,
scripture blaring from the hill.
Press releases in the rubble
humanize the overkill.

Vivisection in the deli,
stupefaction in the dirt.

Maxed out narrative conventions,
metaphor on red alert.

What ghastly limerick's supplanted
haiku, ghazal, villanelle?
Mediocrity in heaven,
vivid excellence in hell.

Gorgon, Grendel, glad Godzilla,
minotaur and loup-garou
rewrite the script of mythic carnage
from the monster's point of view:

an epic of extinction,
a libretto of demise,
a tragedy of oceans,
catharsis in the skies;

a prosody of pleasure,
a rhetoric of rue,
an avalanche's clemency—
oblivion, to you.

Baroquely bloody, stomach-churning,
madly plotted—what about?
Pathetic perils of that ingénue, our planet.
So sad to die and miss the dénouement.

30 SECONDS OVER TOKYO

> *It would be nice if you could just ravel out into time.*
> —Darl, *As I Lay Dying*

In the war room
it's war
that smiley face.

Trot out the bludgeons
have the flung
skulls discuss.

Hard men
get right down there
in the meat.

They hoot
at our ginger
slaughter.

The kid
gnaws dirt in her cellar
and is French

so trumps
the Japanese
whose marvelous hair

went rootless
like heart–tufts
of artichoke.

Dogged
Cunning
Eviscerate
Barbaric

They're holding hats to the fire.
They're selling us down the drain.

Bones away
yell the boys
of my childhood.

~

If I slice my own throat cleanly,
I'll cauterize the fear.
The scar should heal
in the shape
of an "arabesque."

~

. . . things girls
can't do
in Afghanistan . . .

~

I just want to know
that somebody
gets home safe.

That the years will be okay
smuggled close
to strife's soft hide.

This way
to the Theater
of Peace.

Everything happens
as if there's
an elsewhere.

ROUT

1.

The killfest hells away.
The henchfolk hench.

Plode the orb, bro—
im- or ex-,
it's work.

Just don't
barge in all anal,
havocless,

the fishing
spree
abort.

O who
will plumb
the gumption?
Sow the salt?

(The deathrill purls
like Brandenburg
all day.)

We're closing
on the entrails.
Mind the stench.

Half a league
half a league
half a league
girlward

2.
See thugged out
Yankee Doodle don
the chador
of the brave.
Draw on
the clotty goregarb,
gouts and gouts.
Invest
the turbaned day.
Tart up the spoils.

> *While there's a lucifer*
> *to light his fag*

3.

The beautiful days
have done us no good.

Year, furl your colors.
Strike your scars.

Oak leaves gang underfoot
(no end so slippery).

Deluded twigs
spring-tip the solstice dark.

Avaunt, senile buds
of Syringa vulgaris,

you send
the wrong signal—

seeing how
the ax is at the root.

Good golly, Miss Molly,
you sure like to bawl—

breathing's charnel mansion
improbably ablaze—

after the ball's
so over

September-December, 2001

AN ARMY OF ONE

Fungible
but fissile.
Girly-burly.

Buns
or gutter,
sniper?

Shoot.
For the
citadel.

NO USE CRYING OVER SPILLED BLOOD

The daffodils of war had to bend
got their blond faces grimy
under a dump of snow

Bodies backed up
in refrigerator trucks
can't take the heat

Regime melt concluded
tulips lift their chic shapes
into something called peace

ASH-WEDNESDAY, ETC.

So what if the world wills wars and I want to sonnet?
Mod robins nest beyond the Arctic pale.
Spring bagpipes bleat. Kaffiyehed honeys twirl.
(My winter habit isn't yet a hit.)
Slamistas cheer for slap-ass poetry.
We tip through burgs where unrelenting pines
veil derelict structures like domestic crimes.
Past Delhi, snow lies combed in sullen lees.
Then home. Some marquee hawks this apple pie:
1. Lord of the Rings   2. Passion of the Christ
3. Dawn of the Dead. *Say what?*
That blue crevasse or bust. *Prepare the sky.*
March panders like a mouth to a dentist's drill.
Supposing (s)he was nailed to the cross for oil?

THE DAMNATION OF JAN

Variations on a theme from childhood

1.
If I'm not careful, you'll fall into hell.
(God is clever, God takes hostages.)

2.
I am small, I am staunch, I am dumb,
I am weirdly in charge.
I am straining and striving
to haul the human plot
back from the lip
of the pit.

Who left me home alone
minding the world?

I think
I felt
it budge.

3.
Eternity's engine
dragging cars of pain.

4.
A loopy guy-god's
spider-dangles.

5.
Has it got a seacoast?
Has it got a scent?
Do they have the vote there?
Might hell
repent of hell?

6.
Can hell be handed down
without a word?

We've doused (they said)
the Old World terror-flame.

Dyspeptic Luther's theses,
sheep from goats,

Thou Shalts and Thou Shalt Nots—
frail bogey-tales for primitives.

Young Hansel and Gretel
are home from the ovens, singing:

Camp Verboten's over,
mean old witch is gassed.

We really weren't
that German to begin with.

They said all this,
but I was unimpressed.

I'd caught perdition's screen test,
watched her twirl

against the firmament
her fissiony parasol.

7.
Has it got a cunt?
It *is* a cunt.

> Abandon
> Hope
> Down
> There

8.

Hell's just a man who barricades his face
and haunts a city block.
A makeshift, boxy bandage warns:
Keep Out! Damned eyes holed up inside.
Perhaps he's tried to booby trap the throat,
the nostril-stoop and canted earwell?
Or does he deem his countenance a threat,
some type of desperado sun,
that he must veil such radiance?
I feign for years on end not witnessing
unheimlich demonstrations on a park bench,
unvoiced raving pinned to fading brick.

9.

The "thousand cuts."

The "red embroidered shoes."

Hell to hell
carpet
bombing.

10.

I've glimpsed it tenderly, in photographs
of the great bone libraries, housed
in thick-walled, crumbling, blue colonial rooms,
their unglassed windows barred with greenery.
Here children play with femurs, vertebrae.
Invent a legacy. Hushed in the stacks,
years past the killing fields, they line up skulls
in fragile families and dance them through a story—
a glancing, whispered draft of *was* and *will*—
ordeal and benison, derived in calcium.

Hell on a quiet day, in a quiet year.

11.

The body
only hurts

a little while.
Hushaby.

The body
only hurts

and then
it stops.

All praise.

12.

Hell, what
do you want
from my life?

(I know:
obedience.)

13.

I cleave to the brave idea
of not torturing the world.

14.

God I can get rid of.
Just the fire keeps coming back.

CLIFF NOTES TO THE BOOK OF REVELATION

- In twilit dawn the demons of occasions

- October opening

- The leaf/cloud ratio tilted

- A thinning clarity

- But what is this "the world"

- That wound both throat and blade

- Where the god-talk escalates in laundromats

- A darker, tough impermanence revealed

- The barky skeleton

- Night's shelf a disked perfection entertains

- When it's already morning somewhere in the sky

- While the brides of the university dip snuff

- While GHOST AND SMARTY ECLIPSE ELECTION

- While skull-faced babies trawl for death-sweets

- While the fist that creams the cradle rocks my world

- (It beggars the burgeoning)

- They're prick and prick on the hustings

- Someone's yelling on his cell about the sex trade

- Or is it the six train

- History hello get the fuck out my face

- The trees are lamps

- Bouquets

- While we're batting a thousand in the negro leagues

- *We're sorry, we're not at home to answer your call. At the sound of the tone, please leave us a brief message and we'll get back to you as soon as possible. And have a blessèd day.*

- Thus spake Broward County

- Thus Miami-Dade

- Abrade with me

- Inasmuch as you won't abide

- It's blingbling at the slow brink for years

- One last mad dash through the rustbelt battlegrounds

- He bears it away like a brain in the pit of his smile

October–November, 2004

ABLATION

A GIFT OF PAPERWHITE NARCISSUS

You've flown
from harmattan
to snow
with pepper
and a cake—

O you
with your
old indigo
your talk of
Akan widowhood—

I've only
potted nature
on the sill.

Forced.
Irresistible.
White.

WHITE AS THE DRIVEN

To the Ice People

1.

Party favors on my shoulders, pale tinker toys
Heavy beauty on the shoulders of the old, broken pines

Forehead itchy with chill encounters
Fields simplified

In my childhood, "it's sticking" meant something
True winter you journeyed to

Yet back of me was all that Minnesota
Somewhere the German language

2.

So cold
keeps standing armies.

3.

They've trotted out the baubles
we're getting scorched by sudden blue,
miniaturized
beneath the clotted boughs,
fern-forested horizons.

Sun throws
quite a shindig
then splits
like a lousy
non-custodial parent.

Think fairytales.
Think Kafka.
The icing on the cake.
Cordoned by fieldstone fencing,
the tiny heaped-up graves.
What daggered prettiness.
All the comforts
of home.

4.

Bleached New England—
drink it black for once.
Do without the Xtian epithets—
unsullied, pristine, virgin,
stainless, pure. *See*
differently.

(But what does it mean
to daughter
this leviathan of blank?
"The whiteness of the whale,"
etcetera.)

Cuneiform pallor's raining.
Where's Africa?
I echo: pale on pale.

5.

Helmets under the tables,
boast of last night's drunk.
They're men. They talk machines,
they rev testosterone sleighs
(the hell with Herman Melville's
nineteenth century problems)
over the spotless breast
of the newfallen whatever.

6.

> *But I retained the landscape. . . .*
> —H. D. Thoreau

Nine days in Plainfield
I retain

> February hijab
> Inundation petrified
>
> The crystalline declensions of a cloud
> Of a white-on-white kaleidoscope
>
> How one size
> fits every interstice
>
> Home where winter's
> penury and penance
>
> we trundle in from Newark
> over the Meadowlands

another nor'easter dusting
the crime scene for prints

The ruts of commerce
scratched like petroglyphs

That prehistoric rock
the deeper fact

then the river

7.

If the drifts of it were language,
the flakes, syllables—

cranked as those winter boys
in their noisemobiles

I scramble the poem
and beat it.

8.

Silence.
Sintering.

WHITE IN THE WOODS

you remain in that skull-white landscape.
                    —Yusef Komunyakaa

The wages of art! A month in an ex-fort on Puget Sound,
my job to write poems on the theme of modern nature.
On the phone I moan to a race man, "It's White
City out here!" But there's coho (wild) fresh daily at the co-op,
a great blue heron on its rock, the small Skokomish Reservation
down the road. Back where I started, I wander, talk back to Thoreau.

Habits of observation Brooklyn-blunted, I'm no Thoreau.
"You spot that otter?" enthuses a walker beside the sound.
No. I carpool to Seattle for another peace demo. Will my plane
    reservation
have me home by war? The Big Apple will mutter, "How healing to
    be in Nature."
Nice that this co-op (where only the chard's rainbow) honors my
    co-op
card. Wide ferries gently ply, my childhood's colors, green and white.

Schmoozing on Flatbush, Louise: "The West's too white!"
(The same could surely be said of queer Thoreau,
who'd look just right between the lacinato and peacock co-op
kales.) Not quite. She really said, "It's not diverse." Which sounds
more tactful. Stop police brutality, then save nature—
that's her take. Antiguan, well-traveled, she footnotes her reservations:

tots in Missoula thought her light brown child must hail from a
	reservation.
Port Townsend's ball field's still "Home of the Redskins": my white
friend Erin would just as soon not tell her Tlingit pal. Nature's
a monoculture; backed by our Trident base, the row
of snowy peaks with European names endorses Captain Puget's
	Sound.
How's this for a topic? "White Settler Culture Goes to the Co-op."

I'm into Evening in Missoula, Louise's brew, another herbal co-op
treat. Alaska's more mixed, I'm told—no reservations
in that state. As dark claims cold gray sand, I ruminate: sound
the depths of a continent like a pond; it can't be white
through and through. Up Hurricane Ridge, the Park Service pares
	Thoreau
into a decorous sound bite, a photo caption. What color was *his*
	nature,

anyway? But I hate this talk of a place-bound, thing-like "Nature,"
clueless as Park Slope's mantra: *How could we be racist? We're a co-op!*
You help me parse our bright disaster, pale Thoreau.
Bitter at logging on old growth reservations,
my brother-in-law deems clearcuts worse than bombs. This as white
bossmen gird to smite the wogs. As usual. Stop, hey, what's that
	sound?

I write you from a downsized, drive-thru nature. Rude
	reservation
fireworks stands and rawer Forks exhort: *Cooperate, stay white.*
How now, Thoreau? The unsustained wink out. They make no
	sound.

PIGS ADVANCE AS ORGAN-TRANSPLANT FACTORIES FOR PEOPLE

—Headline, *The Seattle Times*, October 22, 2002

Power to the people—
did I really yell it? And, going whole hog, *off the pig!*—
in my salad days, an organic
soybean eater, greenest of greenhorn transplants
from the suburbs, dying for a role in some advance
guard or other, AWOL from the knowledge factory.

I know I took a job in a donut factory,
like an old-time *narodnik*, "going to the people."
Better, I thought, than whoring for an advanced
degree, though I still felt complicit in my civilization's pig-
out. Chairman Mao had the poets making bricks, transplanting
rice, which earned him raves in the underground organs.

"I believe I have injured an organ,"
fibs the doomed grandmother in that factory
of existential yuks, Flannery O'Connor's transplanted
passion play, the one about the people
who get offed on their vacation. Her homespun Pyg-
malion, aka the Misfit, pumps spiritual advance-

ment from the barrel of a gun. My fiction class (advanced)
panned the plot (heavy-handed). A good cadaver organ's
hard to find, the *Times* explains—and look, a pig
has penned a spirited defense of factory
farm techniques. "I believe I have injured the people,"
blurts a shamefaced government, and orders a transplant,
stat. Facelift? Honey, save up for a cranium transplant.

I believe I have injured my planet. Your advances
underwhelm me. How come they say "the people"
when they mean the prosecutor? Don't go postal, organ-
ize. (First find where NAFTA's stashed the factories.)
The small-island child who loved the fried blood of pigs

now cooks with tofu, tempeh, TVP. PETA's pig
supporters gird for a melee with relatives of transplan-
tation hopefuls on Astroturf behind the bioethics factory.
It gets so complicated. What means this verb "to advance?"
Do monkeys hit glass ceilings doing gigs with organ
grinders? That's the trouble with you people.

You toss some token pig a six-figure advance
for her saga of transplant hell; you gobble ribs, bacon, organ
meats. You hesitate: are women fetus factories or people?

CRITTER

East

Beside a pond chartreuse with algae
like indoor-outdoor carpeting

the sinewy cyclist gripped a ringing fish—
no: a silvery cell phone.

~

"Pacific Northwest? It must be
beautiful out there."

~

Did somebody mention
a visit to Shark Cathedral?

~

I'll tear you apart like a fish,
yelled Franz's father.

West

Drift limbs ricked in the old way.
Cold beach   foggy gravel.

Tide currents drive
like a river in that sea.

Ocean self   tree self.
Anadromous hecatombs.

I'll tear you apart like a fish,
yelled Franz's father.

~

18, 20 whalewatch boats
per orca.

A job or a critter?
Which?

~

Clubbing hatchery salmon
on the Methow

from a pristine
point of view.

~

Stumped? Just cuff
yourself to the mast

and chant: coho/aluminum
coho/aluminum.

At tether's end, inquire:
What would Kafka do?

THE STRAITS

> *Swim*
> *and you are not in your country.*—Richard Hugo

1.

It's always
been
about edges

snowberry
Nootka
rose

stranded
kelp orgies
fly-visited

some collective
swerve of
sea life

12,000 years
since glaciers
took a powder

old beaches
hoisted
above us

sandy
birdy
autumn sedgy

lichen fruiting
all over
island rock

madrone's
fall fettle
blazing like Malinche

sunlight dragging
a pale sleeve
across bluffs

Pacific
rimming
the skyboys

2.

afternoon in an
SUV with relatives
chasing the elemental

talk out here's
of Costco
and toxins

cloperylid
sushi trays and
creosote

drunk Seattle
mothers hunkered down
in the 1950's

"I almost got
a goat in
San Francisco"

Dick Hugo's wave-
stopped bleak
gussied with gadgets

RVs called Lakota
rigged
for satellite

days of
advection fog
and gorgonzola

to each
white town its
"friendly" Indian

"so many fish
right now people
getting kinda crazy"

where's nature
are we
there yet

3.

world comes down
with its dark
over diligence

all falls
let it fall
away west

singly kindle
land lamps
and sea lamps

up Whidbey
and whale-
raked Haro

a fool
and his folly
are soon

leader
follow
the breath

it's always
been
about edges

old cold salt
inhuman
tides

those great
liquid
roads

if you
like
difficulty

SE FUE LA LUZ

I.   *an enormous*
       instantaneous
       reversal
       of the power flow—The New York Times 8/16/03

in the blink
of an edge
on a sun
carved
afternoon

whizzed back
to cavey life—
                              se fue
    but vertical!   se fue
                              not peter
                              ing just
                          split

       a total
       eclipse
       of the civ
       o bang
       on pots
       to bring
       it back   the hot
                        guttering
                        skirl the
                        fueled
                        bray what

68

music
we're
inside of

se fue
la luz
por qué

because the
parce que
took a hit

(some
vast *they*
appeared to
screw up
royally

night
& the
lampless
homestacks
hunkered in
chopper thud

we scuttled
in ginger
lightlack
like some
techie deity
was shining
a flash-
dark on us

Washington
Heights sent up

that old Caribbean
refrain

       (it happens
all the time
as in: back home

   (aleatory?
sure, that's
half the fun

         se fue
              se fue
      la luz

II.   *huge amounts*
of [your
identity]
that had been
moving east
over the Great
Lakes suddenly
sucked back—The New York Times 8/13/03

on the brink
in the black
of an eye
the system
booked

       (possibly whacked
by shoulder-
fired
missives

            (it happens
        all the time
        as in: Accra

no water
and no lift
on the 13th
floor

                or:

                urge
                and demi-
                urge went
                down
                to the
                brook

                            (could not
                        pull off
                        the spontaneous
                        sparkle bit

a well
no not
a net o
not a
safety
anything

                in the run-up to
                deep-seated
                jitters &
                blahs

                            71

we
clambered
through silo
blackness
down
and down

                        (it happens
                all the time
                as in: Najaf

containment
unit-like but
plumbable

        gripping
            a candle
        stub

                        (it happens
                all the time
                as in: Dhaka

then door gaped
splitting
hallblack
with that ax
of cheery sun

        to hope
                to pray
        to ope
                that can

of worms
all pillowy
& couchy
bourgeois
apartmented

(as if
peering into
an extinguished
a dismembered
wayoflife

& so
her case
"went death"

their list
of don'ts
included
do-rags

(lupus
and buboes
both   what
else can go
wrong

III.   *The world, as viewed by the newly appointed dean of*
Yale Law School, Harold Hongju Koh, is divided
between darkness and light. . . . [A]s a member of the
Clinton administration, he joined Secretary of State

Madeleine K. Albright on a trip to meet the North
Korean leader, Kim Jong Il. "The moment I remember
most was when we flew out of North Korean airspace
and into Seoul, we left a land of darkness and suddenly
there were all these lights," he recalled. "I mean it
was just brilliantly lit, and as we got closer there was
all this teeming activity and I said to myself, 'This is
what democracy means.'" — "Battling the Darkness,
with the Law as His Lamp," *The New York Times* 11/11/03

demo
crass
see
reboots

tho'
raggedly

      your identity
is back:
traffic lights!

               your identity
      is back:
               hygienic whirl
of excrement!

      your identity
is back–
               D batteries!

your identity
is back:
                exhaustless
ranks of

grooming
        products!

your identity   ,
went black
        now it's

                        back

aquí
la luz
resumes

        the vasty
blaze

from here
        to entropy

                that drone's
                the johnny
                one note
                lullaby

                the AC
                August
                hymn

                of sub
                atomic

                    particles
working
on a
chain
gang

IV.   *[The bio*
         logical
         tocsin
         ticks]
         for thee–John Donne

          but
        which co-beings
                    didn't
have a blackout

consider:

          dragonfly

or
                    shadow
          of leaf
     on leaf

cloud
          on cloud

                                how
            the bright
   plunge
                        of a bee

eschews
                the grid

heart
    vine
  decants
        each night
one long
        cool drop

                tree lean
            against
        the blue
    why

the aspirined
                            blood
of the
                sun

                (having gone
to the expense
of having
                                continents
in the first place

ABLATION

1.

She speaks of what happened here
in the Pleistocene.

2.

Little black dresses with bun wraps.
Mom's tattoo.

Wife-beaters spilling cleavage.
Razor wire.

3.

Rapt bays.

A memory
of butterfly on rock.

4.

In the Land
of Throw-Away.

5.

Within stillness, sound
from a ship across water.

6.

Versions of history—

"The Yakamas grew warlike."

7.

A red ship is passing silently,
white sail against its flank.

8.

"She was ovulating
but I was working."

9.

The settlers grew peacelike?

The settlers grew alfalfa.
Speaking evermore of *empty lands.*

10.

A rabbi is sounding a shofar on the front step
of the correctional facility.

11.

A chair marooned in the garden's
now a bucket.

Happy rain.

12.

At 8:46 the first_____
struck the north_____.

13.

Claw inside a shell
groping out.

Mapping glaciers'
ablation areas.

14.

So I behaved well.
Or badly.

15.

Climbed

up

some.

16.

Screaming mother tore
upstairs locked

bathroom door
turned on that

real terrible gas
was it 1934.

17.

Slim names grooved
in clay crumblebluffs.

The blue waterways
where kelp gardens fatten.

18.

Scruffy ideograms
of Doug fir against gray.

19.

"I won't follow you off
the cliff you liberal lemmings."

20.

Oh great river
elided.

21.

Slated
for truckling.

22.

She worked tirelessly
and stupidly for peace.

23.

"Put up a headstone for your mother
before you can't find her grave."

24.

Beseeching
and besieging.

25.

"Going all around the world
helping people

who don't know how
to brush their teeth."

26.

Machine generations rest
rusting

in this fucked pasture.

27.

Peacelike.

If not peace.

28.

Another hill: another sky

29.

Ripped teens rapping
down the hot dark.

T-shirts rolled
to armpits.

Peoplescapes.
Boy nipples.

War here
and there.

30.

So much to be gathered
about the dwindling.

31.

The waving of self
over a field of_____.

32.

Well it's that
or burrow into

hardest nature

a fastness
of rock   of star.

NOTES

"Ghazal: Happenstance"
    The line "*Did you ever dream lucky, wake up cold in hand?*" is from a
    traditional blues.

"The Fate of Forms"
    BMA: Brooklyn Museum of Art.

"Rout"
    The line "while there's a lucifer to light his fag" is a slight revision of
    a line from the World War I-era song "Pack Up Your Troubles."

"White as the Driven"
    The town of Forks, on Washington State's Olympic Peninsula, was the
    epicenter of the late twentieth century "timber wars" in the Pacific
    Northwest.

"Pigs Advance as Organ-Transplant Factories for People"
    PETA: People for the Ethical Treatment of Animals.

"Critter"
    The line "I'll tear you apart like a fish" is from Franz Kafka's
    "Letter to His Father."

    "Clubbing hatchery salmon on the Methow"
    On the Methow River, in eastern Washington State,
    fish managers ordered the destruction of hatchery-reared salmon
    thought to be competing with endangered wild fish stocks.

Born and raised in the Pacific Northwest, Jan Clausen has lived in Brooklyn, New York since the 1970's. She is the author of the poetry collections *From a Glass House* (IKON) and *Duration* (Hanging Loose); the novels *Sinking, Stealing* and *The Prosperine Papers* (both from Crossing Press); and a memoir, *Apples and Oranges: My Journey Through Sexual Identity* (Houghton Mifflin). Clausen has received writing fellowships from the National Endowment for the Arts and the New York Foundation for the Arts. Her book reviews and essays have appeared in *Boston Review, Kenyon Review, Ms., The Nation, Poets and Writers,* and *The Women's Review of Books.* Clausen teaches in the Goddard College MFA Program and at the New School. Her work is available at www.ablationsite.org.